HANSA

HANSA

The True Story of an Asian Elephant Baby

Clare Hodgson Meeker

**With Photographs from
Woodland Park Zoo**

Illustrations by Linda Feltner

SASQUATCH BOOKS
SEATTLE

The amber-eyed calf makes her entrance.

A BABY ELEPHANT IS BORN

Early one November morning at Woodland
Park Zoo in Seattle, an Asian elephant named
Chai rocked from side to side on her huge
legs. She was about to give birth to her first
baby. "Steady, Chai. Good girl," said
keeper Russ Roach, quietly reassuring
her while the other keepers swayed
back and forth with Chai in silent
unison. If the keepers were
anxious, they tried not
to show it.

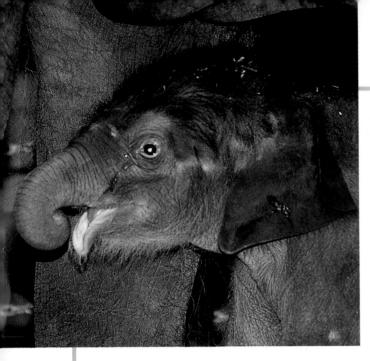

No elephant had ever been born at the zoo in its 100-year history. Would the calf be born alive? Would Chai accept her new baby? After two years of waiting, they were about to find out.

As soon as the calf was born, the keepers rushed in and pulled it away from Chai's feet, but kept it within sight of her. Because Chai had never given birth before or seen a newborn calf, the keepers were not sure how she would react. They had heard sad stories from other zoos about mother elephants trampling their newborns because they did not know what they were.

The zoo veterinarians cleaned the calf off with a dry towel and recorded its weight, a healthy 235 pounds. They had known for some time that the new baby would be a girl. Meanwhile, Chai snaked her trunk in their direction, sniffing the air for information about the new arrival.

Within a few minutes, the little calf lifted her head up. Her 10-inch trunk, looking small for her face, hung limp as she struggled to her feet. Slipping a nylon strap under the calf's belly, two keepers helped her walk toward her mother, while another keeper filmed her taking her first wobbly steps.

Left: The baby has to figure out what to do with her trunk.

Right: The newborn gets a helping hoist from keepers Chuck Harke and Don Bloomer.

Packy Facts

"Pachyderm" is a term that refers to elephants and other thick-skinned, hoofed mammals. Elephants' large toenails are considered hoofs.

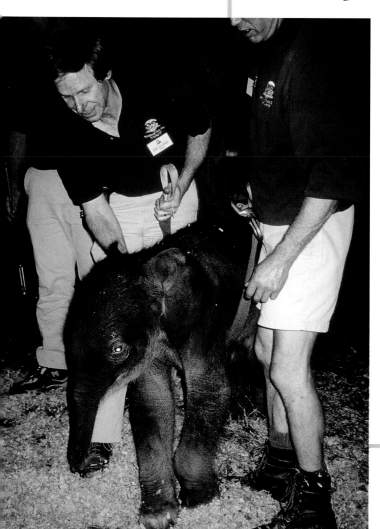

Suddenly, Chai uttered a sound like a deep, rumbling roar. Was she calling her calf? The keepers stayed calm but alert. They had to be careful with this first introduction. The calf inched closer. Chai reached out and gently sniffed her all over with the fingered tip of her trunk.

Everyone in the elephant barn breathed a sigh of relief. "It's a miracle," said lead elephant keeper Pat Maluy, feeling the hectic 22 months of preparation and worry melt away as he watched Chai bonding with her newborn calf.

"I'm a grandfather," said retired keeper Tommy Wood. He had raised Chai since her arrival at the zoo in 1980 as a one-year-old calf and was back to help with her new baby.

When a baby elephant is born, it cannot take care of itself. It needs its mother and the other female members of the herd to care for it. A calf learns by imitating its mother and aunties. In the wild, female elephants grow up watching over younger calves in the family herd. However, none of the elephants in the zoo's all-female herd had ever had a baby before. How would they react to the new calf?

The keepers placed the other elephants in separate stalls in the barn during the birth. Thirty-one-year-old Watoto was put in the stall closest to Chai's. An African elephant with tusks, Watoto was born in the wild and is the herd's leader, or matriarch. Nine years older than Chai, she had always acted protective of her. When Watoto saw the calf for the first time, she lowered her head and studied her newest charge, eye to eye.

Twenty-one-year-old Sri, an Asian elephant, was also nearby. The keepers wanted her to see a birth so she would know what to do when she had a calf of her own. "Motherhood is learned to a degree, even in the wild," said Tommy. "Elephants watch others in the herd and learn from that." Sri was more nervous and excitable than the rest of the herd. When she saw the calf coming toward her, Sri quickly retreated to the far corner of her stall.

In the stall farthest from the birth was 34-year-old Bamboo, another Asian elephant and the oldest member of the herd. Smart but moody, Bamboo could sometimes be aggressive. The keepers thought it best to wait a little before introducing her to the calf.

Packy Facts

Elephants do not sweat in order to stay cool. Instead their extra-baggy skin, with all the wrinkles, increases the surface area of the skin and keeps the elephants cool. African elephants have more wrinkles than Asian elephants because they live in a hotter climate.

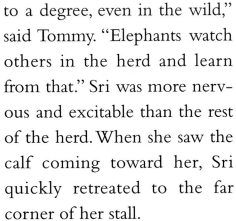

Left: The elephant barn's official greeter, under her mother's watchful eye.

Half an hour after birth, the baby elephant walked by herself. Sniffing around her mother's legs, she picked up the scent of her mother's milk and started to make sucking sounds. At first, Chai nervously shifted back and forth on her feet. She seemed confused about what to do until Russ gave her the command to move her front leg forward so the calf could nurse.

Above: At first, keepers Pat Maluy and Tommy Wood give the newborn calf a wooden platform to stand on so she can nurse.

Right: Within days, the baby can stretch her neck to nurse without help.

But the calf could not reach her mother's breasts. She was still too stiff to lift her neck and stretch. Seeing the problem, the keepers had a platform built to boost her up for the first few days. Standing on the four-inch-high platform, the calf latched on with her pointed tongue and took her first drink.

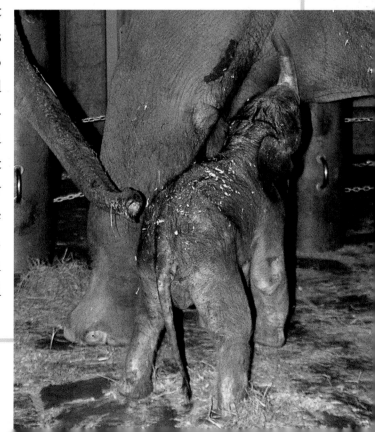

LEARNING THE DAILY ROUTINE

For the next month, the five keepers worked around the clock in shifts to make sure Chai took good care of her baby. The calf nursed in short spurts of no more than a minute, but she nursed often. Every day, she drank nearly seven gallons of milk and gained almost three pounds. "Chai was a milk machine," said Russ. The keepers fed Chai extra hay and grain throughout the night to keep her strength up.

Elephants normally sleep at least four hours a day, but sleep was a rare event for Chai. Whenever she tried to lie down, the calf would nudge her to get up so she could nurse again. Even when the keepers commanded her to lie down, Chai stood up as soon as she heard her calf's nasal squawk.

The busy calf sometimes fell asleep standing up. The keepers would see her start to tilt and have to help her lie down. With her tongue hanging out, the calf would groan and twitch in her sleep. Then suddenly she would jump up and run to her mother, as if she had been frightened by a bad dream.

Chai was a very attentive mother. If the calf strayed away, Chai would follow her or anxiously sway back and forth until the keepers steered her back. It was exhausting for everyone keeping up with all the activity. But when their shift was over, the keepers found it hard to go home. "I don't want to miss anything," said Russ.

At one week old, the calf is small enough
to hide underneath her mother.

It was important for the calf to learn the daily routine, starting with the morning bath. All winter long, while cold rain drummed on the roof of the elephant barn, the temperature inside remained a steamy 75 degrees, thanks to heat pipes and bright lights mounted high in the wooden rafters. The morning was usually the most relaxing part of the day for the herd and their keepers, a time of soft voices and close contact. But it was hard to relax with a month-old, 300-pound calf on the loose!

The keepers took turns hosing down Chai and her baby with warm water. As the amber-eyed calf raced by, they had a few seconds to scrub the bristly hairs on her back with a metal brush. Though small compared to her 8,400-pound mother, she was still dangerous, stumbling around on unsteady legs. "Like a bowling ball, she could mow us down like pins if we weren't alert," said Tommy. Dodging the hose, the baby would run under her mother's legs to hide. Then she would toddle off again to explore her world, while Chai kept a watchful eye on her.

As the calf grew stronger, the keepers began to take her outside in the afternoon with Chai and Watoto. Watoto was careful to avoid stepping on the

Packy Facts

The wooly mammoth, closely related to the present-day elephant, roamed North America nearly 2 million years ago. About the size of an Asian elephant but with a stockier body and shorter back legs, the mammoth also wore a thick coat of hair to protect it from extreme cold during the last Ice Age. Its spiraling tusks grew as long as 16 feet. It is thought that the wooly mammoth became extinct due to overhunting and sudden climate change.

calf as she ran back and forth between the two grown elephants. She gently blocked her with her foot when the calf tried to run underneath her, and swatted her if she played with Watoto's tail. Chai did not mind Watoto's scolding. Her baby needed to learn to get along with the rest of the herd.

Bamboo and Sri were not yet allowed outside with the calf. "We wanted them to be either positive or indifferent to her before proceeding," said Pat. So far, they did not get along with her.

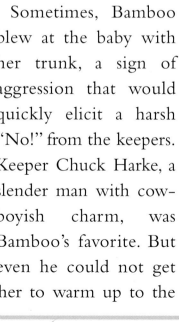

Above and right: Sweep off the hay, rinse, and scrub. After a warm bath, the baby will follow keeper Russ Roach anywhere.

Sometimes, Bamboo blew at the baby with her trunk, a sign of aggression that would quickly elicit a harsh "No!" from the keepers. Keeper Chuck Harke, a slender man with cowboyish charm, was Bamboo's favorite. But even he could not get her to warm up to the

Packy Facts

The scientific name for the Asian elephant is *Elephas maximus* or "biggest elephant," although the African elephant is actually bigger. While an Asian bull can grow to be 11 feet tall, an African bull can be as tall as 13 feet.

Left: The calf quickly bonds with her "Auntie" Watoto and runs back and forth between her and Chai.

Right: The baby likes spending time with Watoto doing what the keepers like to call "quality pestering."

calf. He tried rubbing peanut butter on the calf's back to get Bamboo to touch her. The sly Bamboo ate the peanut butter but ignored the calf.

Sri still acted afraid of the calf. The keepers tried introducing Sri to her in the yard just outside the barn. As soon as the calf started to run under her legs, an instinctive act to feel close and protected, Sri got spooked and hit her with her trunk, sending the calf rolling. The baby would have to learn to slow down and walk at an elephant pace before Sri would accept her.

Some things happened that were not part of the daily routine. In January, it snowed. At first, the calf was hesitant, but soon she was running, stomping, slipping, and sliding in the snow and eating the snowballs the keepers gave her. In February, she felt her first earthquake. As the exhibit windows rattled in their frames, the elephants trumpeted together. The calf ducked for cover under her mother's legs. A minute later, when the shaking stopped, the elephants quickly settled down again.

There were so many noises to get used to. The first time the calf heard the keepers roll the wheelbarrow in to clean the barn, her ears flared and her tail stuck

Packy Facts

Throughout Asian culture, the elephant has long been revered as a symbol of intelligence, grace, and power. In India, the elephant has played an important role in all aspects of daily life: work, religion, myth, and royal ceremonies. In Hinduism, India's most common religion, one of the most popular gods is Ganesh, the elephant-faced god who symbolizes new beginnings. In Thailand, where Buddhism is the major religion, people believe that the Buddha was a white elephant before he was reborn as a man. The white elephant is rare and therefore highly regarded and considered the exclusive property of Thailand's king. It is not actually white, but a light gray color with big patches of pinkish pigment on the forehead between the eyes.

straight out in surprise. But the voices of zoo visitors, already a part of her life, did not seem to bother her.

The baby elephant was a media sensation. Television stations, newspapers, and magazines across the country carried stories of her birth. With only a few baby elephants born in North America each year, the calf was now a celebrity. Thousands of people waited hours in the pouring rain to catch a glimpse of the four-legged toddler running, stumbling, nursing, and playing. "She gave a whole new meaning to the word 'cute,'" said Tommy.

By February, the calf was three months old. It was time to give her a name. The zoo held a contest and chose the name Hansa, which means "supreme happiness" in Thailand, the country where Chai was born. From the smiles she brought to visitors' faces, it was clear that Hansa's name fit her perfectly.

Left: When keeper Don Bloomer takes Chai and Hansa outside, Chai must walk carefully to avoid stepping on the calf.

Right: Seven-year-old Madison Gordon celebrates her winning name for the baby elephant.

1:30–3:15pm
Walk, play, and graze outside in south yard.

3:30pm
Drink and swim in outdoor pool.

3:45pm
Walk back to barn.

L.M.Feltner

8:00am
Keepers arrive and
clean barn.

9–10:00am
Elephant training in
barn with carrot
treats.

10–12:00pm
Baths and foot care.

4:00pm
Feed on grain.

5:00pm
Hay put down for
the night.

8:00pm
Feed and rest in
separate stalls.

CHAI'S PREGNANCY

The keepers had always wanted Chai to have a baby. The problem was that Woodland Park Zoo had no male elephants with whom Chai could breed. At 19 years of age, she would soon be too old to get pregnant. So the keepers decided to send her to Dickerson Park Zoo in Springfield, Missouri. An Asian bull elephant there named Onyx was Chai's only hope for having a baby.

"Every elephant birth is important," said Woodland Park Zoo veterinarian Dr. Darrin Collins. Elephants are already endangered in the wild, and the elephants in zoos are getting older. Unless more elephants are born in zoos, experts predict that there may be no elephants left at all in 20 to 30 years. The keepers knew it was a risk sending Chai 3,000 miles away to Dickerson Park Zoo. But she was in good health and had a calm, stable personality. Of all the elephants in the herd, they felt she could best handle the journey.

For several days after Chai had left for Dickerson Park Zoo, Watoto, Sri, and Bamboo charged out to the south pasture, where she was last seen, to look for her. They called out with noisy clucks and rumbles, clearly missing their friend.

Chai was driven by truck, with two keepers following behind in a car to make sure she was safe. She spent the entire 60-hour journey swaying back and forth in her crate and refusing to eat or

Chai gives a salute before leaving Woodland
Park Zoo.

drink. As soon as she arrived at Dickerson Park Zoo, Chai was introduced to the 11,000-pound Onyx. The keepers returned to Seattle with good news: the two elephants got along famously. Within six months, she was pregnant and ready to come home. But by then, summer had arrived in the Midwest. It was too risky to drive her back in the heat. Chai would have to wait until fall to come home.

Chai spent a lonely summer without her family. She could not stay with Onyx. Male elephants can be very aggressive, and the zookeepers did not want to risk injury to Chai. And she did

Left: Even-tempered Onyx, Dickerson Park Zoo's Asian bull elephant, turns out to be an ideal mate for gentle Chai.

not get along with her female roommates. Elephants live in a society based on rank, with the powerful elephants in a herd dominating the less powerful ones. At Woodland Park Zoo, Chai had always enjoyed a high rank because of her relationship with Watoto, the leader of the herd. But as the newcomer at Dickerson Park Zoo, she ranked at the bottom of the herd and was picked on by the other females. Luckily, several young calves were attracted to the expectant mother, so at least she could practice her mothering skills.

Hearing that Chai was not eating well, the keepers had her favorite kind of hay, timothy grass, shipped to her. When they

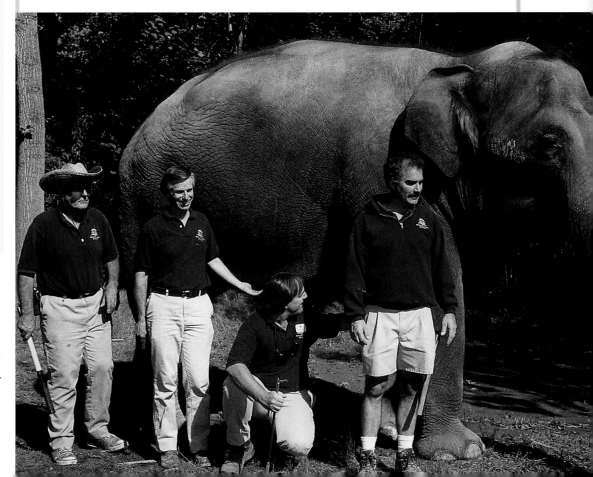

Right: Keepers (from left) Ken Morgan, Don Bloomer, Pat Maluy, and Russ Roach watch over a pregnant Chai.

arrived in the fall to take her home, however, they were surprised to see that she had lost 1,000 pounds during her stay. The keepers were not worried, though. Chai had been overweight when she left for Dickerson Park Zoo. Her new weight would likely keep the baby smaller and make the birth easier.

Chai must have recognized the keepers when they arrived from Seattle. With no hesitation, she followed them into her traveling crate. Remembering her first trip, the keepers did not expect Chai to eat much on the way home. But she proved them wrong, feasting on whatever treats they found for her at roadside rest stops: cantaloupe, watermelon, cinnamon bread, and 16 boxes of Pop Tarts.

Packy Facts

Elephants may seem slow-moving, but they cover a lot of ground. They often walk six to nine miles in a day and can run up to 25 miles per hour!

Left: A happy reunion with Chai and her extended family: (from left) Sri (pronounced "see"), mama Chai, Bamboo or "Boo," and Watoto or "Tote."

Right: Home again outside Woodland Park Zoo's elephant barn, which is modeled on Thai architecture.

Elephant Artists

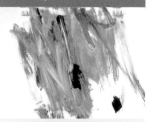

In the wild, elephants have been known to etch markings in the ground using rocks and sticks. At the zoo, the keepers give each elephant a brush filled with paint and let them go for it! Bamboo curls her trunk around the brush in a tight grip and layers paint on the canvas, while Sri holds the brush loosely. Watoto prefers a sponge or a wide-handled brush and applies the paint delicately. Chai prefers not to paint at all.

If Hansa were given a brush filled with paint, she would probably try to eat it!

Upon arriving home after a year away, Chai was quickly reunited with her family. One by one, Watoto, Sri, and Bamboo greeted her with flapping ears, lots of rumbling, and squeaks of excitement. "You could tell they were happy to see her," said Pat. Adding her own bark to the noisy celebration, Chai was clearly happy to be home.

WHAT IS A TRUNK FOR, ANYWAY?

When Hansa was born, she did not know what to do with her trunk. She would shake it around or fling it over her shoulder to get it out of the way. Sometimes she put it in her mouth, like a child sucking her thumb. She had to learn how to hold it up so she and the other elephants would not step on it.

An elephant's trunk is the most important part of its body. With over 100,000 muscles in it, the trunk is strong enough to lift several thousand pounds, yet delicate enough to pick up a feather. It is mostly used for nonstop sniffing: finding food, smelling danger, social touching, making sounds, and drawing up water.

Russ gave Hansa toys to play with so she could practice using her trunk. She had a soft, blue rubber ball to toss up in the air and a black bowling ball to roll around the floor. Her favorite toy was a rubber tub. She would squeeze her body into it like a snug play-house and drag it around with her wherever she went. "But she could have fun without any prop at all," said Russ, "just running around in circles with her imaginary friend."

Within a few months, Hansa showed better control of her trunk. During the morning bath, she drank water from the trough or slurped it up from the floor and blew it into her mouth. Outside, she tried to throw hay and dirt on her back, imitating the way Chai dusted herself to keep cool. When she did not aim high enough,

Sometimes Hansa curls her trunk in her mouth,
like a child sucking a thumb!

Packy Facts

An elephant eats
300 or more pounds of
plants and fruit a day and
washes it down with 60
gallons of water! However,
only half of what they
eat is digested.

Left: A mass of pink freckles between her eyes is Sri's distinguishing feature.

Right: Hansa plays hard with her inflatable exercise balls and soon wears herself out.

the dirt ended up in her face. A few sneezes, a shake of her head, and she was back at it again.

Hansa could be very persistent. One day, Tommy watched in amazement as she figured out how to unlock a metal clip on one of the chains the zoo used for babyproofing. These chains, strung between metal columns, or bollards, were supposed to keep Hansa in the exhibit but give the keepers a way out in case they had to make a quick exit.

Unlocking clips was a dangerous game. From then on, the keepers would have to be even more watchful.

Hansa already had learned a few simple commands, such as "Come here," and "Back," but the one she heard the most was "No!" Like any smart animal, she tried to see what she could get away with. "Elephants love to learn," said Tommy, "and you've got to 'think elephant' to keep up with them."

Left: A hairy tail makes an excellent fly swatter!

Right: As long as Chai can keep her in sight, Hansa is free to roam in her outdoor world.

Elephant Teeth

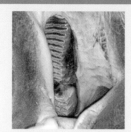

An elephant grows six sets of teeth over its roughly 60-year lifespan. Shortly after birth, two molars appear on the upper and lower jaw with a second set forming in the back of the mouth. As these molars wear down, they are pushed out by new and increasingly larger sets of teeth, which can eventually reach a foot in length! When the last set wears down, the elephant can no longer chew its food and dies. Tusks are also teeth. These incisors, made of solid ivory, continue to grow throughout an elephant's life. The longest tusk recorded was 11½ feet.

DANGEROUS WORK

By early spring, Sri and Bamboo were clearly losing patience with the change in routine caused by Hansa's birth. Although the keepers trusted Watoto to be around Hansa, they were still afraid that Sri and Bamboo might hurt her. Used to being outside much of the day, regardless of the season, the two elephants now had to wait until Hansa could be safely separated from them. They also missed the attention of their favorite keepers, who had to devote more time to supervising the baby.

The keepers did not feel good about the way things were, either. Russ missed giving demonstrations with Sri before a crowd of zoo visitors. "It's the most amazing feeling, working with an elephant," he said. "You don't even notice the people. It's just the two of you communicating by subtle body movements. That's all that exists at that moment."

Watching Sri pace nervously in her stall and refuse to obey commands to lie down for her bath, Russ worried about the change in her behavior. "Consistency is key in working with elephants," he said. No longer the youngest elephant in the herd, Sri was probably confused about her ranking position.

Bamboo was also acting out. She tried to grab a keeper's ankus, a wooden tool used in elephant training, and knocked another keeper down while he was sweeping up hay. This is why there are always at least two keepers scheduled to work at the same time, so they can back each other up in case of trouble.

Keeper Ken Morgan, shown here with Watoto,
demonstrates the mutual respect between the
keepers and their elephants.

Left: Keepers Chuck Harke and Don Bloomer take Chai and Watoto for a swim in the pool.

Right: Watoto's strong and knobby trunk can quickly block a running Hansa.

Protected Contact

Caring for such a large, intelligent, and potentially aggressive animal makes the elephant keeper's job one of the most dangerous jobs in America. At least one keeper is killed every year in zoos around the country. As a result, many zoos are moving to "protected contact," redesigning exhibits to limit direct contact with the elephants in order to prevent keeper injuries. Zoos are still learning about how these changes will affect the relationships between keepers and their elephants.

For 10 years, the keepers had worked together with this herd, bringing a wide range of experience to their jobs. Ken Morgan had no illusions about the dangers involved in this work, having had an elephant knock him down and even try to swallow his head when he worked in the circus in his early 20s. "I can tell you there is no air in an elephant's mouth," said Ken, "and

Left: Like mother, like daughter: Hansa imitates Chai's walk as they explore the yard.

Walking on Tiptoes

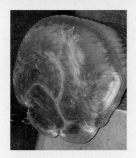

An elephant actually walks on the tips of its toes. Thick padding around the toes and heels cushions the elephant's weight, allowing it to walk through the forest on sure and silent feet. At the zoo, foot care is a very important part of the keepers' daily routine. Hoof knives and filing tools are used to trim nails and pads, clean off dirt, and smooth out cracks on the bottom of the feet to avoid infection.

The keepers have to check Hansa's feet while she is asleep because she is ticklish!

their saliva will make your eyes sting." Having learned from that terrifying experience to be more alert and assertive, Ken was now one of only three keepers who were allowed to work with Bamboo.

There are times when the keepers need greater control of the elephants' movements. For bathing, foot care, or medical attention, the elephants wear leg restraints for their own safety, as well as for the safety of the staff. Keeper Don Bloomer practiced putting a bracelet on Hansa's foot for a few minutes each day. "It's like having a leash for a dog or a bridle for a horse," he said. Even though at five months Hansa was still a baby, she was also a 500-pound wild animal who did not know her own strength.

As long as the keepers work in close contact with the elephants, it is important that they be considered dominant members of the herd. "An elephant's instinct is to respect dominance," said Don. For example, Bamboo never challenged the matriarch Watoto, even when Watoto bullied her. Bamboo knew better than to tangle with an elephant that had tusks. But as the dominant members, the keepers were responsible for the elephants' safety. If the change in routine made Bamboo nervous, it was up to the keepers to reassure her.

This raised another worry in the keepers' minds. If Hansa were in danger, would Chai come to her defense? "She might expect us to defend her instead," said Tommy. The only way to restore peace to the herd was to help Bamboo and Sri accept Hansa.

BREAKING NEW GROUND

Chai had been a doting mother for four months. More relaxed in her role, she no longer followed Hansa around constantly. Hansa was growing bolder by the day and began to reach out to the rest of the herd.

One rainy afternoon in March, Hansa was in the barn with Chai, separated from Bamboo by a "howdy" wire, an electric wire that gives a mild shock if touched. The keepers had just finished cleaning the barn and had gone to their office in a back room to do paperwork. A video camera mounted in the barn allowed them to keep track of what the elephants were doing from their office. Everything looked peaceful. The elephants were resting.

Ten minutes later, the keepers looked up and saw Bamboo standing right next to Hansa, with no hot wire between them. There had been no unusual noises, no snorting or blowing or stomping the ground, the usual signs of trouble. Bamboo and Hansa just stood there together. Chai had not uttered a sound.

The keepers quietly went in and separated the two. "Bamboo must have stepped over the wire," they said later. What could have been a disaster turned out to be an important step forward: a positive encounter between Hansa and Bamboo.

As spring gave way to summer, the elephant forest turned a lush green. Clusters of bamboo and big, leafy spikes of purple flowers created an exotic setting for Hansa's outdoor antics. At 800 pounds,

First two feet, then four, then her head, and
finally her whole body: It took a week for
Hansa to get used to deep water.

six-month-old Hansa had the run of the pasture. While Chai and Watoto grazed on grass, Hansa preferred dirt. Picking up and throwing dirt was normal behavior for an elephant, but eating it was not! After several bouts of diarrhea, Hansa was grounded in the barn for a few days.

Sniffing around the barn one day, Hansa discovered a hole under the door to Sri's stall. Suddenly, Sri's trunk appeared in the hole. Hansa laid her trunk on top of Sri's, and for several minutes their trunks touched in a sign of greeting.

The keepers tried putting Sri in the same room with Hansa, separated by the "howdy" wire. Continuing to explore each other over the wire, they linked trunk tips as if they were thumb wrestling. Then Hansa stuck her trunk in Sri's mouth. "I'm not sure," said Russ, smiling, "but it looks like a sign of affection."

An unusually warm July gave the elephants the chance to indulge in their favorite cooling-off activity. An 11-foot-deep

Packy Facts

Elephants make good neighbors in the wild. They make paths, knock down fruit and trees, clear land, and spread plant seeds through their constant eating. Because they change their environment in a way that benefits other plants and animals, they are considered a "keystone species."

Left: Once Hansa is in the water, it's hard to get her out. Chai lays down to wash off the dust before returning to the barn for the night.

bathing pool outside of the barn was the perfect spot for Hansa to test an elephant's love of water. Elephants are natural swimmers. Using their trunks as snorkels, they submerge themselves in the water and swim up to 20 miles at a stretch in the wild.

Every day, in the middle of the afternoon, the keepers took Hansa, Chai, and Watoto to the pool on their way back to the barn. At first, Hansa did not want to go in. The keepers led Chai into the water and hoped Hansa would follow. Instead, Hansa dipped one foot into the water, and then quickly retreated to Watoto, who was standing beside the pool.

Gradually, Hansa grew braver. Seeing her mother lying in the pool, waving her massive head around, Hansa dunked her head in the water, too. Then came her feet and finally her whole body. With legs pumping, Hansa galloped through the water, lurching her head up and down to breathe. The keepers themselves got a soaking as they bribed Chai with carrots to stay in the water so that Hansa could practice swimming.

Elephant Talk

Elephants are very social animals. You can hear them trumpet, squeak, and rumble to each other. But acoustic biologist Katharine Payne recently discovered they also communicate by "infrasound," low frequency sounds that can't be heard by the human ear. In the wild, elephants use infrasound to keep track of one another over long distances.

Each vertical line represents one octave.

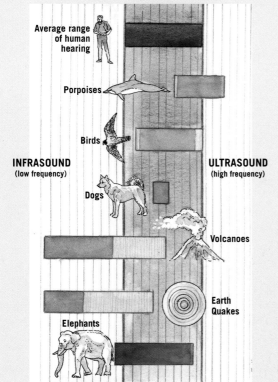

Average range of human hearing

Porpoises

Birds

INFRASOUND (low frequency)

ULTRASOUND (high frequency)

Dogs

Volcanoes

Earth Quakes

Elephants

PART OF THE HERD

By late August, 10-month-old Hansa weighed 900 pounds. She was now gaining only a pound a day, probably because she was always on the run. As soon as the keepers opened the barn doors, Hansa would take off outside. Like a child at recess running to grab a favorite swing, Hansa would rush over to her rubber ball in the south yard, give it a push with her trunk, and kick it around the grassy field while Chai and Watoto grazed.

Bamboo was now able to join them outdoors, though she tended to graze off by herself. This is normal behavior for Bamboo. "She always was a loner," said Tommy. To Hansa, Bamboo was another warm body to be near and play with. Sometimes Bamboo allowed Hansa to sniff around her legs before gently guiding her back to the group, nudging her with her trunk. But she was also quick to let Hansa know when she was bothering her, by trumpeting loudly and pushing her away.

Unfortunately, Sri was still skittish around the baby. They were visiting well over the "howdy" wire in the barn. But the keepers still remembered Sri being spooked by Hansa's running. They wanted to wait until Hansa slowed down before allowing the two elephants to be together outdoors.

The keepers mingled playfully with the herd. One day, Chuck took a seat on the blue ball, waiting to see what Hansa would do. Making it clear that she did not want to share, Hansa backed up and pushed him off with her big rear end.

Hansa uses Auntie Watoto for a scratching post.

Visiting on a late summer day, observers might notice the brown hair on the elephants' backs glistening in the sun, a reminder of their woolly ancestors. They might see Watoto reach up with her trunk to tear a leaf from an over-hanging tree, towering over them at close range. Sniffing the air and the people curiously, her enormous trunk would make a sound like a wind tunnel or the distant ocean in a seashell.

It is hard to imagine that one day Hansa, too, will stand huge and magnificent. Elephants have roughly the same life span as humans, continuing to live and grow for 60 years or more. The keepers plan for Hansa to live a long and healthy life at the zoo with Chai, Watoto, Bamboo, and Sri.

In a year or less, Hansa will stop nursing. She has already started adding grain, carrots, and hay to her liquid diet. When she reaches adulthood, Hansa will be the first elephant ever born *and* raised at Woodland Park Zoo. Perhaps one day she will have her own baby and bring new hope to the endangered Asian elephant.

Above and left: African elephants like Watoto have "baggy britches" and long eyelashes to protect them from the hot sun.

Right: At one year of age, Hansa is comfortable hanging out with Watoto and Chai as well as the more reclusive Bamboo.

Comparing Asian and African Elephants

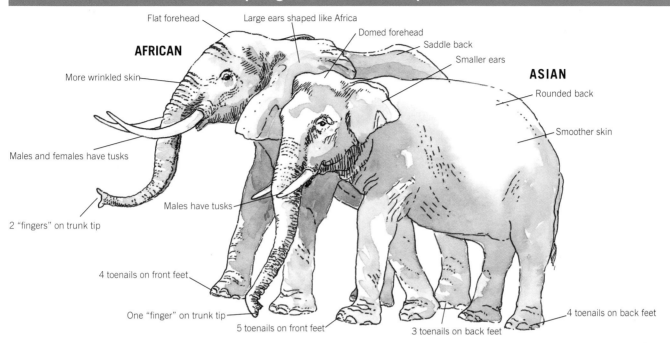

AFRICAN

Flat forehead

Large ears shaped like Africa

Domed forehead

Saddle back

Smaller ears

ASIAN

More wrinkled skin

Rounded back

Smoother skin

Males and females have tusks

Males have tusks

2 "fingers" on trunk tip

4 toenails on front feet

One "finger" on trunk tip

5 toenails on front feet

3 toenails on back feet

4 toenails on back feet

Left: Someday Hansa will walk at an elephant's pace, but for now she enjoys being young.

Saving the Endangered Elephant

Of the 600 elephant species that once roamed the earth, only two remain today: the African elephant (*Loxodonta Africana*) and the Asian elephant (*Elephus maximus*). Today, even these two species are in danger of extinction. Roughly two-thirds of the elephant population has disappeared from the forests of Asia and the grasslands of Africa. Decades of war, explosive human population growth, and expanding cropland and cities have displaced elephants from their natural habitat. In the 1970s, over half the African elephant population was slaughtered by ivory poachers. Even with laws outlawing international trade in ivory, there are still countries that would like to see the ban lifted and the legal sale of ivory resumed.

As we begin a new century, it is clear that humans hold the power to protect or destroy the environment and its inhabitants. It was largely public pressure that brought about the world-wide ban on the sale of ivory. Conservation efforts are now underway throughout Africa and Asia to teach lawmakers, land owners, park and wildlife officials, and volunteers how to protect endangered elephants and balance human needs with the need to preserve habitat.

Across the United States, zoos are striving to create a more natural environment for the animals in their care. This gives the public the chance to learn about elephants, as well as their natural habitat. Woodland Park Zoo has joined other zoos in participating in the American Zoo and Aquarium Association's Species Survival Plan (SSP), which coordinates breeding efforts to preserve and protect zoo animal populations. Hansa's successful birth represents ten years of coordinated effort by Woodland Park staff and elephant reproduction specialists across the nation. These efforts are helping to revive the endangered elephant population.

It is said there are three categories of people: those who make things happen, those who watch what happens, and those who ask only after the fact, "What happened?" Which one will you be?

Woodland Park Zoo

Partial proceeds from the sales of this book will benefit the Woodland Park Zoological Society. Hansa is the first elephant born in the Woodland Park Zoo's 100-year history. The zoo is an award-winning institution, whose more than 300 different animal species attract one million visitors a year. It's also home to 35 endangered and five threatened species. A model for zoos across the nation, Woodland Park was one of the first to create innovative natural habitats and is a leader in promoting conservation and education.

Resources and Helpful Web Sites

The following organizations are working to save elephants and other endangered species and habitats:
Care for the Wild USA, PO Box 46250, Madison, WI 53744, www.cftwi.org
Friends of the Earth, 1025 Vernon Ave NW, #300, Washington, DC 20005, www.foe.org
World Wildlife Fund, 1250 24th St NW, Washington, DC 20037, www.wwf.org

Other Helpful Web Sites

http://natzoo.si.edu The National Zoo has a new male Asian elephant baby named Kandula born
    November 25, 2001.
www.elephants.com The Elephant Sanctuary is a natural habitat refuge for Asian elephants in Tennessee;
    their web site provides additional information on elephants.
www.zoo.org Woodland Park Zoo's web site has information and video footage on Hansa and elephants in
    general, as well as on the zoo's conservation efforts.

Additional Reading

Elephants Calling, Katharine Payne (Crown, 1992).
Elephant, Caroline Arnold, photographs by Richard Hewett (Morrow Junior Books, 1993).

Acknowledgments

Special thanks to Woodland Park Zoo's elephant keepers Chuck Harke, Russ Roach, Ken Morgan, Tommy Wood, Don Bloomer, and Steve Cremer; veterinarians Dr. Janis Joslin and Dr. Darrin Collins; and Senior Keeper Helen Shewman and Zoological Manager Pat Maluy at Disney's Animal Kingdom for graciously sharing their time and expertise.

I would also like to thank the Woodland Park Zoological Society and the Woodland Park Zoo staff for their cooperation in arranging the interviews and photographs for this book, particularly Bruce Bohmke, Terry Blumer, Gigi Allianic, Ric Brewer, and Wendy Hachnadel. Additional thanks to Melinda Mancuso at Dickerson Park Zoo for providing the photograph of Onyx.

Thanks also to my agent, Michele Rubin, my editor Kate Rogers, and the staff at Sasquatch Books for their persistence and enthusiastic support of this project.

Dedication
To Russ, Chuck, Don, Ken, Tommy, Steve, Helen, and Pat for
teaching me how to think like an elephant, and to my family for giving me
the time and the wide open spaces to write.

Printed in Singapore by Star Standard Industries Pte Ltd.
Distributed by Publishers Group West
09 08 07 06 05 04 03 02   5 4 3 2 1

Cover and interior design: Karen Schober
Cover photograph: Art Wolfe
Interior illustrations: Linda Feltner

Photographs in this book were provided courtesy of the Woodland Park Zoo and the following photographers:
Kaye Cartwright-Lissa: pages 4, 6, 8, 9, 11, 13
Dennis Conner: pages 27, 28, 29 (right and bottom), 30, 33, 34, 39, 40, 44, 46
Agnes Overbaugh: pages 1, 2-3, 14, 15, 16, 21, 23, 24, 29 (top), 31 (large), 35, 36, 43, 45
Russ Roach: pages 7, 31 (small), 37
Dickerson Park Zoo/Jeff Glazier: page 22
Woodland Park Zoo: pages 17, 25

Library of Congress Cataloging in Publication Data is available.
hardcover ISBN 1-57061-344-3
paperback ISBN 1-57061-370-2

Sasquatch Books
615 Second Avenue
Seattle, Washington 98104
(206) 467-4300
books@SasquatchBooks.com
www.SasquatchBooks.com